Scrap Rat

Written by Clare Helen Welsh

Illustrated by Irene Montano

Collins

Stan has some card and some pens.

Snip!

Stan has a pot and some clips.

Stick!

Scrap Rat runs to the sink.
Stan yells, "Stop rat!"

Scrap Rat runs on. His ear comes off.

Scrap Rat jumps in the sandpit.
Fliss yells, "Stop rat!"

Scrap Rat jumps high. His tail comes off.

Scrap Rat runs into Wilf the cat.

Scrap Rat is torn!
Stan has a plan.

He gets pens, clips, card and a pot.

Scrap Rat has his ears and tail back!

Wilf the cat is back too ...

Stan map

🐾 Review: After reading 🐾

Use your assessment from hearing the children read to choose any GPCs, words or tricky words that need additional practice.

Read 1: Decoding

- Practise reading words that contain adjacent consonants. Look through the book. What words can the children find that have the adjacent consonants "s" "t". (*Stan, stick, stop*)

Read 2: Prosody

- Model reading each page with expression to the children.
- After you have read each page, ask the children to have a go at reading with expression.
- Look at page 4 together. Model using expression and a voice to read the speech bubble.
- Talk about how we might read sentences with exclamation marks.

Read 3: Comprehension

- Look at pages 14 and 15 together. Ask the children to retell the story using the pictures.
- For every question ask the children how they know the answer. Ask:
  - What is Scrap Rat made from? (*string, card, paper, glue*)
  - On page 7, why does Fliss yell at Scrap Rat? (*he is splashing sand at her as he jumps*)
  - What happens to Scrap Rat's tail? (*it falls off in the sandpit*)
  - Who rips Scrap Rat up? (*the cat*)
  - What does Stan do when Scrap Rat is torn? (*he makes another one*)
  - What scrap animal would you make? What materials would you use?